Big Fantasy Coloring Book in Grayscale

By Molly Harrison

Fairies, Mermaids and Witches

This coloring book features 100 pages of grayscale images - all images from *A World of Fairies*, all images from *Autumn Magic*, all images from *Enchanted Sea* and several images from *Fairy Coloring Book in Grayscale*.

www.mollyharrisonart.com
© Molly Harrison 2019 All Rights Reserved

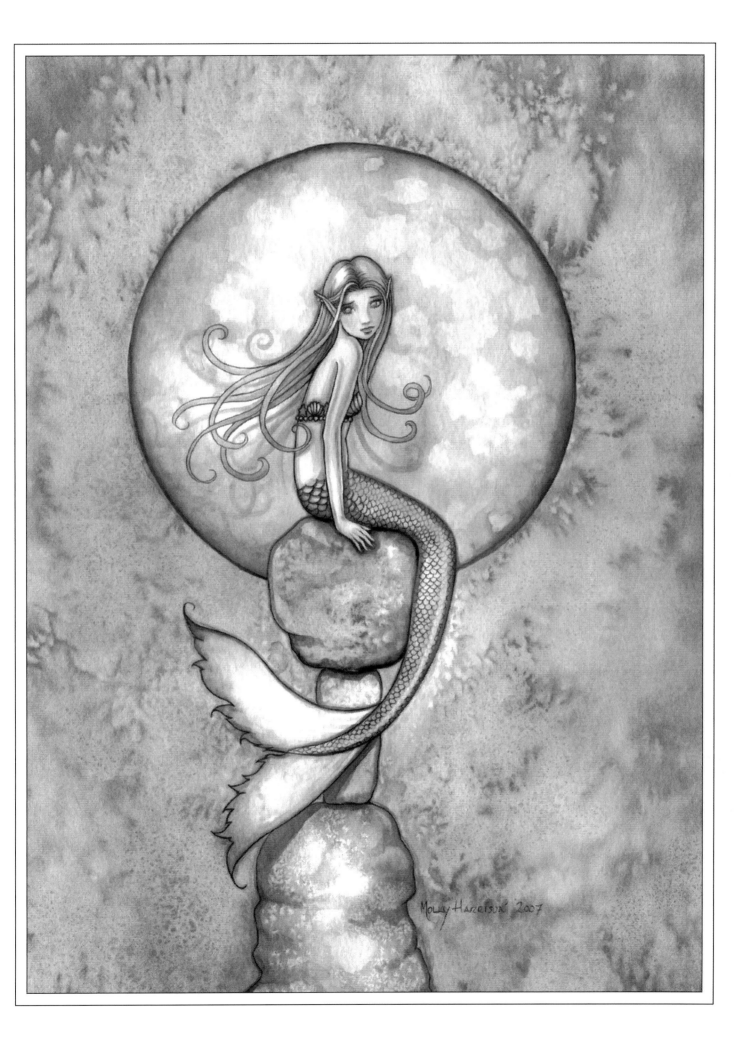

Made in the USA
San Bernardino, CA
03 June 2020